Una visita a/A Visit to

La granja/The Farm

por/by B. A. Hoena

Editor Consultor/Consulting Editor: Dra. Gail Saunders-Smith

Consultor/Consultant: Jennifer Norford, Senior Consultant
Mid-continent Research for Education and Learning
Aurora, Colorado

Capstone
press®

Mankato, Minnesota

Pebble Plus is published by Capstone Press
151 Good Counsel Drive, P.O. Box 669, Mankato, Minnesota 56002.
www.capstonepress.com

1 2 3 4 5 6 12 11 10 09 08 07

Library of Congress Cataloging-in-Publication Data
Hoena, B. A.
    [Farm. Spanish & English]
    La granja = The farm/por/by B. A. Hoena.
    p. cm.—(Una visita a/A visit to)
    Includes index.
    ISBN-13: 978-1-4296-0082-8 (hardcover : alk. paper)
    ISBN-10: 1-4296-0082-9 (hardcover : alk. paper)
    ISBN-13: 978-1-4296-1192-3 (softcover pbk.)
    ISBN-10: 1-4296-1192-8 (softcover pbk.)
    1. Farms. 2. Agriculture. I. Title. II. Title: Farm. III. Series.
S519.H5718 2008
630—dc22   2006100178

Summary: Simple text and photos present a visit to a farm—in both English and Spanish.

Interactive ISBN-13: 978-0-7368-7911-8
Interactive ISBN-10: 0-7368-7911-0

Editorial Credits
Sarah L. Schuette, editor; Katy Kudela, bilingual editor; translations.com, translation services; Eida del Risco,
    Spanish copy editor; Jennifer Bergstrom, set designer; Kelly Garvin, photo researcher

Photo Credits
Bruce Coleman Inc./IFA-Animals, 11
Capstone Press/Gary Sundermeyer, front cover (cow), 1, 4–5, 8–9, 12–13, 15, 16–17, 18–19, 20–21
Corbis, front cover (crops); Macduff Everton, 7
Digital Vision, front cover (barn)

Pebble Plus thanks the Minnesota Agricultural Interpretive Center, Waseca, Minnesota, for the use of its farm
for photo shoots.

Note to Parents and Teachers

The Una visita a/A Visit to set supports national social studies standards related to the
production, distribution, and consumption of goods and services. This book describes
and illustrates a visit to a farm in both English and Spanish. The images support early
readers in understanding the text. The repetition of words and phrases helps early
readers learn new words. This book also introduces early readers to subject-specific
vocabulary words, which are defined in the Glossary section. Early readers may need
assistance to read some words and to use the Table of Contents, Glossary, Internet Sites,
and Index sections of the book.

Table of Contents

Tabla de contenidos

The Farm

A farm is a fun place
to visit. Farms have buildings,
fields, and animals.

La granja

Visitar una granja es un paseo
divertido. Las granjas tienen
edificios, campos y animales.

4

Farm Buildings

Barns are large buildings
where animals live.
Barns also hold crops
and equipment. Farmers
milk cows in barns.

Edificios de la granja

Los establos son edificios grandes
en las que viven los animales.
En los establos también se guardan
la cosecha y las herramientas. Los
granjeros ordeñan las vacas en
los establos.

Bins hold food that
farm animals eat.
Bins are round and wide.

Los graneros guardan la comida
que los animales de la granja
comen. Los graneros son redondos
y muy amplios.

Farm Animals

Chickens look for food

around the farm.

They peck at the ground.

Animales de la granja

Las gallinas buscan comida

por toda la granja.

Picotean el suelo.

Sheep graze. They eat
the grass in a pasture.

Las ovejas pastan. Comen
pasto en la pastura.

13

Pigs stay in their pens.

Pigs snort and squeal.

Los cerdos se quedan en
el chiquero. Los cerdos
gruñen y chillan.

Fields and Crops

Farmers use tractors
in their fields. Tractors
pull heavy machinery.

Los campos y la cosecha

Los granjeros usan tractores
en los campos. Los tractores
jalan máquinas pesadas.

Farmers drive combines.
Combines help farmers pick
or harvest crops in the fall.

Los granjeros manejan cosechadoras.
Las cosechadoras les ayudan
a recoger la cosecha en otoño.

A farm is an important place. The food people and animals eat comes from a farm.

Una granja es un lugar muy importante. La comida que comen las personas y los animales viene de las granjas.

Glossary

barn—a building where animals, crops, and equipment are kept

combine—a powerful vehicle that picks or harvests crops when they are finished growing in a field

field—an area of land used for growing crops

graze—to eat grass that is growing in a field or pasture

pasture—the land that animals use to graze

tractor—a powerful vehicle that has large wheels; tractors pull farm machinery, hay wagons, and heavy loads.

Glosario

el campo—área que se utiliza para cultivar la cosecha

la cosechadora—vehículo de mucha potencia que recoge la cosecha cuando ya está madura en el campo

el establo—edificio donde se guardan los animales, la cosecha y las herramientas

pastar—comer pasto que crece en los campos o en la pastura

la pastura—lugar que los animales usan para pastar

el tractor—vehículo de carga que tiene ruedas muy grandes. Los tractores jalan las máquinas de la granja, los vagones de heno y las cargas pesadas.

Internet Sites

FactHound offers a safe, fun way to find Internet sites related to this book. All of the sites on FactHound have been researched by our staff.

Here's how:

1. Visit www.facthound.com

2. Choose your grade level.

3. Type in this book ID **1429600829** for age-appropriate sites. You may also browse subjects by clicking on letters, or by clicking on pictures and words.

4. Click on the **Fetch It** button.

FactHound will fetch the best sites for you!

Index

Sitios de Internet

FactHound te brinda una manera divertida y segura de encontrar sitios de Internet relacionados con este libro. Hemos investigado todos los sitios de FactHound. Es posible que algunos sitios no estén en español.

Se hace así:

1. Visita www.facthound.com

2. Elige tu grado escolar.

3. Introduce este código especial **1429600829** para ver sitios apropiados a tu edad, o usa una palabra relacionada con este libro para hacer una búsqueda general.

4. Haz un clic en el botón **Fetch It**.

¡FactHound buscará los mejores sitios para ti!

Índice